The North Road Songbook

The North Road Songbook

Verity Spott

Remark on the Air

It's a clear night, mid-October, and the first real cold
has fallen around the city; the air I spoke of, clear,
quiet species presents itself. Forty four windows
faced ours, and our lamplight signed the divide.

The Contents

The North Road Songbook

(2019-2023)

On Jasmine
for Megan

She washed eleven leaves and thought of her sister.
In the nearly detailed day in the crook of the moon
she makes her hours, ties a ribbon around her waist
and the sky deletes the roof commands

the air to a halt, and you are sad.
But listen little sister we're going to Ithaca soon
in the dawn of our dreams the hermitage sky
of exhaustive moons I will put on my hair

and go on strike again. And the strike will be
for the dead of each hour and I tremble with fear
when I speak my words are scratching the sky
and leak as I helplessly stir in the water.

Eleven rotates, of our tiniest days, the palaces sway
and the huge collapse of the furnace, the arcane
flume, the watertight doors icumen to the stoop of a sea.
The wands await, she said, and the evening flowers away.

Night Seen at Burnham

First, there's a single light,
then a pleiades alone deep in
the dark but the focus clears
reflected on a lifebelt

and the mooring figures gathered
at the edge of what you know is the dark
water frozen sodium sky, come here
to the inlet look, what is it empties

and fills, passion, but obsession.
A sense of the slump in the night
little shapes dormant carriers,
but obsession, it returns predictable

as leather in the backbone,
quiet fixation ruled by the order
look out, back to the finish that night
mooring squares into focus.

Bus Stop Diner

A sleepy knot in the boiler room, still
the feeling of a diner comforts the one
we found in Harlem sitting in a booth
waking or sleeping the doves

began their strange looping song-
like in that refrain two have, three have passed
not to alarm you but we're bleeding and this
gentle composure, come out of the cupboard,

please, my God what's happened to us
you're shaking I'm totalled two hundred and forty
care hours thrashed the liver pale
and the pigeon is stuck with its neck in the glass...

...and then, thunder from a car,
something, such specific comfort
in these places, the nameless of it all, the endless
seam, the menu, I'll have some combination

knotted to adjoin: My heart to yours, my
when I am sleepless riven depth
in an upset sun he was on his bike, really
he was so alone you should have seen him flower.

The Dunes at New Brighton

A dent in the floor of the world.

You moved the dial with your hand.

How much hurt, and we were held into the moon
rise and framed. So how much hurt

never new answers peppered the speech

the sun appeared and we were lined
on the dune, tussocks arrested
but stop shouting the relief
in reflexive laughter.

No more mercy. Self realisation;
the horrible lie in the schema
I look out over the fells,

to Ireland, past the windfarm.

There is a furious king in the dunes
the people I love so much
the trying is the matter
can barely stop thinking, one single problem.

For everything out before the windfarm
heart of tussock hearts.

Crocus Meadow

It was exactly here, at this bench
where Frankie wrote

St Ann's Well Gardens, and you missed them
terribly. Now exactly here I returned

that feeling, the bank or bench I tried to find
along the Lewes Road my head scrambled
that part of town

I lived at another. It always felt as though
we were housed at distant ends

of a tunnel, surprisingly near, to miss
that feeling closeness. Heart

of a certain world.

Some tinnitant map
in strips sleet blue
sentiment changed
course took you
to the electric
bathroom
you were in pain
 why have you
brought me here
the window look
at the flickering city
all of its failing raids

Relatively Peaceful

Remember blue light
will steer
    bodies
alive
    bodies
that your hands
    already, come to
life rejected helpless
our family preference
as brain
    blood
is spilled
    he is not
good
    in love
    divine is
hymns and dancing.

Another Late View at the Harbour
for my family

There's a bright white glare to the right
do you see it the tingling flash of a
dinghy proof if needs be there's
some ovation round the lock, and here

almost moth-like, the teething problem:
Settled to move I regained my strength, and
in the light that is pierced... There's many
I have done the wrong thing thoughts

cluttered round the outlet at low tide purses
unclaimed but not a shattered boneyard like one might believe,

believe, in the troubled dusk the pipes seem to moan
little by little losing anchorage you flowed, or,

you floated away. You float away.
In the distance the flats and the hard are each the same.

If You Love Me Remove Me

Warrants concoct electrical
work the rescue alarm
bells tring tearing
agape a low pain moves

through years
officer informant speaking
whether it be murder jail
or frisking the terms of

debate no longer exist you don't
get to feel you're gone
I heard a cry a fine
is a murder is a crime.

and these sparrows sing
one note again and again
in the garden under public
view black eye sweet smell
I've tried to track; honey, strong
in evenings' avenue
a butterfly a white admiral
drives my heart by light caught
to think of all those people
with you last night my mouth

full of blood nettles all around
and progeny these flowers split
not a betrayal dreams
of perfume underwings dog fight
sparrows depart but I faltered,
they came back, and the garden
mutters the volta lost city lost
garden sisters plaiting
flowers and for all of the
insects, hi, and rob the hand.

for Rob

Chapter House

To be trained sick with doubt
put you across
to the unpleasant matter
of naming, and she became

bright by day by day eating
forgetting to pray, but to seek out hearts
was enough, became too clear

sky above troubled
ever so
evensong, lectures on the common law
broadcast for radio forget

them too, not being unkind
but die than be that ministry.

...

heavy rain from the west
hammered the window.

Clear sky, it means
are you managing to rest? Is the pain a little
quelled? I would have said

I will come to you soon.
It is impossible.

A very few streets over,
it is my job

to help you
through the city.

Roof Terrace

It's difficult to speak

tears over the street

graves and pavement chemical

stains I saw you move

a creeping minute strewn

rust and daisies high

enough to hide us.

after John James

to love the same records
drinking the shade
of the dress life is wearing,

it's almost as though this deliberate
vagueness, dreamlike in
detailed fantasy, when forms broke down...

...rain across the valley blurred the air
from my Hollingdean window

down the sparrows, cruel rain
settled to the language of contract.
Provided the rain stops

may I meet you in the hotel with
yellow borders, green shutters, lay
down at leisure, piss each other off.

A Pretty Photo

Unable to pass all red
flown detail statin slow from the neck
that a hard day falls gulp our shadow

stoop at last, relief to take
my breathing, so light we go
dying all away down

the jaundiced moon. Scattered
china imagine being that soft
nukes the morning frost.

Dye me dear officer heels
on the wretched curb, sick
fizzing through the planes. A heap

of dung passes slowly down
each of the city streets can you
hear it, my darling? Our
day too appears.

Receiving Live Foods in Cold Weather

The dream gauze of
friendship the contrail
up to the clock tower stupid,
indifferent, transfixed. What I love

she said as she sucked her partner's tongue
is abandonment loosed from them all:
The skirt length propagandist, our lady
of the seating plan by the dark fire lit

grief riven cellular clutch me
I'll dart away close off the face
in the quiet room where I cut him.
But all was dead flat grey, unreason
neither cut nor clung; an open
responsive echo closing down.

Goodbye, I wave the marina
pale food sermon
disappointment in the hall. But
still leak song, the medal

I kept in my pocket when you'd gone
I sang silent in the brain whirred
limbs lit stimulant detail
sailing through and out along
the holy blood.

At 6 some sun appeared, marked for a moment's sky
I thought of a house of God, on strings

I thought of a moment the sun was there
a strange light a ship in the sky

we were sinking thought at 6 some light
in passing panic in sky a heightened ship ship ship

Aubade

Morning strikes a bizarre warmth
climbing out the window the nib
lifted the skin like a glove

in this old bed staring
at the ceiling for moments entirely
blank on where I am, haunted

we departured, hard and forever
after such fill on life by side
and gone to our stations.

Then the difficulties, chipping,
climbed onto the roof for an escape
suns up harsh on where you're gone.

From Jew Street to the Foundry

We'd into the world the screaming feet of
geese flight from a sky would burn here stop.
Soft our dappled frequency. We'd sit as if
already bond, supposed work these

accomplice burners dark and it is stop. It is
Wednesday attacked we go held to speak, ship
against the grounded, in the foundry on fire, destroyer

as if in no-place would burn; here to speak to go
to the second rate work, stop. Homeward bliss
to slip in the hatch and dissolve to nightshade, Ship!
Reluctantly to sleep then to accrue the vicious day.
The sinking sailboat of our ship, Wednesday

back for you we go another way. In case the hissing town-
street, ship, stop on ice. There is a jut.
There is a beauty graves the middle of the week, is now on fire!

Meet, well met unallowed so not too out, to ship the burner.
Now for the jetstreams, ghostship, joke shop manacle esplanade:
The present day gone past to find away, a cute come back
Wednesday come back Wednesday come back Wednesday.

Steady the snow isolate
gorgeous through the blood
to see how far

how close we could come
North Road I'm given
to think of

you there, one house
and roofs over and over
most if not all

that does not claim to warm
sirens through the blood-
dry stone.

Somewhere north of here there's a Hill,
I wonder. The moment
has been prepared for.

Orasaigh
for James

& so there is being born
it stutters into view

finds that the sea it is,
an expensive colour.

I wore my pretty skirts
& played in the lochs

& meadows
were my sweetness

sung she was loud & un-
gainly. The sky pierced

the clouds were
all around, hazard fades

I must wear grey (as the
wind catches) & gently peeled

away. There is a clean day its
airs sing you come alive.

O LORD but I have been, no.
She will neither listen or die, not yet,

the tender
delights of the day in grey
I will wear my heart for you

& softest tulle.

A world is clearing. Under the heat
of the light she lets her hair

& the icy water floats
& gapes apart.

I've caught some fish,
and the quiet inlet dipped
adonis blue.

& we will eat, and she

can sing, ever soft in the wilds
of a world there is a flower

tall above the crushed moss
in mute white her purples
as veins O LORD,

whatever has she done.

& if she worked the sky with echoes
if she dared to stay outside

if her pretty skirts they
danced for you or dared
to brush her face.
Then the skin & teeth of the sea.

Who is this girl who LORD,
will not announce her quiet,
dreams sincerely, wears a lilac tongue,

(if a day comes back
arrested,
& confiscates her dawn).

It is a filthy thing this
toying in the detail.

a magpie moth is come, O LORD,
to wrestle out her eyes
& she is fiercely danced
in lilacs, tulles & floating
out the year.

(O, LORD, the things I've done
she said, believe, the things
I've done. I have drowned my long
grey skirts, I have torn away
my headpiece, made merry of a bunny
clutched in claws; I have felt
my way through the field, a dot
on the horizon of eternity).

Antihistamine

and as it cleared that you lay
      to scatter by me, to dream,
            fever, to copper the sky,

which stars; its body
      or clears the bridge
            that is a beating rest, which lay

in a beaten rest to the bridge,
      the dream that cleared to copper
            the stars and poisoned sky

in a heat denied to sleep
      and dream to the steer,
            so lay by heat to clear.

The Sanctuary

There's something I've been trying to access
a particular point in feeling. There's the difficulty.
It's attached to conditions at points
along the curvature. Words when they come
stare him straight in the face, as if he were the centre
though perhaps he was the background
the music falls on. He was the kind of man
you would follow into the loss of return.
You would not. Only a clod would enter that trail
but I get to see them: My own footprints in the rain
spilling out nonsense en route to the City.

Next there's the door salesman that took out the rest of your life
people said you're not in danger, passing through
the phased exit. Listen, Fauntlaroy, you can pay me back
whenever, the next mass suicide event
you had blood pissing down my arms. We were so unwell.
In the shop window there was a model of a skeleton
for anyone that needed to get a skeleton.
The crosshairs moved away, so locate it again:

On the wall behind The Duke we were frozen
puppies forbidden lightness kissing
this aubade simply gorgeous, banned at ease.
In the ABBA cafe life prevailed. One hundred years ago
the boundaries raced beyond this station,
The Regency estate blunted to the west with brickwork
and a road, a wide, gaunt avenue of sadness.
So it's time to turn away once more
to the corner feeling almost complete
obliteration and how stupid again to be that way moved.

All the while he stood there developing a doctrine,
soap products, card games, asking for everything I shouldn't have
had for free. Somewhere else for now, a little way off
west on the beach at high tide (the mast of the wreck
twitching in the drink) you won't want to do this anymore,
you said, in a year or so, and there it fired up
the flickering tongue that takes you down to the Sanctuary,
how old, I'm in the same place and have moved
and remained the present tense folded, stupid
to the pressure you're inside it: A different kind of risk.

Villa Kaliopa
for Dolly

If I could take it
    away from you

the fields should sing
    that our eyes are set

on a balcony, far off
    we heard for love

so if I could take
    or mend, and then

to send... That the sorrow who spoils
    at an edge,

for us all, but most to you
    whose pang will not allure

the sharp wall
    our garden...

There are things I could give
    and must be slightly still

the garden, lung or sky
    torn into

for the most of all our dreams,
    so I fell to sleep

I wake I fall I stand I fear
    I sleep

I fall I fear I sleep
    I dreamed

in the garden I fell
    and deeply sense of our love.

& if we had two streams
I would drink wine with you
& grill a fish, tempt out
the waving lizards
I want it to rain
and stay indoors today
quiet together, and later on
a few hundred miles away
in a walled garden
careless as sparrows...

Postscript, on North Road

The clarity of silent cold
all alone shapes hung distinct

without breath the sea even is
I imagine flat and voiceless

charm trembles its terror
that you do not and choose

to couple. One night there I
went to the stuck open

window with you in my hand light
flickered grotesque and you said why

have you brought me here?
So I took your head

outside into the air the city
glimmered as still water to the flat

of a hand and though an autumn
settled and we had missed the call

woken up so sad, surprised by
sadness too we were able to see

calm distinct the city light
colours breathing

that what it meant was I am unsure
this particular stillness

and inside its little cabin secret
histories,

just one moment just
a little hinge in the night to come that night

did fall, and our eyes
are rearranged...

...so the pattern, what we found here ghostlike
total calm may hold

sheer lovely, threat too. They are
non-distinct, here again

the night takes me to stare out,
poised, raise a little signal

mute unthreaded cold across
the city speaks, and glimmer to the touch.

Late Night Poem

That your children meet the day
in the new world banned music

even the timber, still, and as ready
I was for you to fall, my darling,

that they go to the schools who are
they now, chutes of love & violent

totally (we know. but are made to watch
again & again what dying away

is) it okay to pull the screen?
I can't bear to see; even friendship

failed so much too remembers
the day snaps it is failed to weep stuck it

goes on: Into the night, but it is still
past paralysis of cells. Quiet, care

shifts knowing there is real
work ahead. It is so vital,

after the one that works in the night
still flat, as all were scrambled to the helm.

Two Cards

Steel away
let's steel
away

low
we stand
beneath a

sky falters.
Let's
be gone

to the low
detail, the
beds rose

kept, lead to
the touch
melts

me my grief
sweet bird
'who's far away'

Lovely
stooping skies
where you leave

the world
away, 'melt
to pit &

to love' are
heard each day
a slight

shade. Too
slow, let's
away so

dear under the
drowned
hills

in their way
toward
my "spirit
passing by"

In a Landscape

A little particular tip of sober light
the lonely hour, to find out

solitude, the room
cleared in a landscape, and I can learn

what you meant: *the soft white
mist blown in from the ocean...*

...and those that have managed
to clear their course

reach out kind, in memento
pledge to gently guide,

arranging the heart. This fairer way;
the stream ahead, white noise

let the quiet night move in,
long, particularly beautiful

the guide hand pentatonic
softly clear in the drift. Think,

the tender precision of thought. Water
curving slate tonight may gesture me along.

Postcards from Berlin

(2023)

All the nerve of leaving
in the sky falls away
like the land.
The great lakes and forests
razored by the autobahn.
Steady pressure as we fell
knots gave way
to excited
corn fields all over
the earth, and to think
you used to order your world
by the way the cranes were facing,
same work different life by degrees
the gentler poisons.

Eating the floorcrusher
light's coming up
a painting
that captures the beauty
of the ocean at a moment
like this well rest
in the sunset's path.
Drop it. Bouncing
mechanic sugar gals
dizzy on two step flight path
high flying right
up to the drop it,
forestation lo pass
high high high high.

and land, hardtech bossman
the plaza is different
in the summer drop
it diffuser varied blood so let
him in left to die little
precincts, hallways stretching
back into who knows
in my dream where you were
the staff nurse, we were dying
cold sweat embarked to romance
the bubbles. To romance the stye.
To romance the chainlink fence.

Alkoholfrei municipal
bed music panora
chime recline alone
its forward birds
trickled wait, wait,
years are going by
by here again to you
uh sorry proud
lit pica journey
to speaking; fill the space
a wasp aboard
the spine and the hum
and chatter and beer
and gravel came awake.

Such was the evening clear
tranquil sound at play
mayflies pas de bourrée, if I could paint this,
frame first the lens impression
would fill, magnolia
fading to grommet blue by dust
chestnuts, linden gals hug out
and a tiny scream, just there
at the top of the image clear
bulbs in lines a harmless scream,
child at play terror
latticed ivy kissing
where the last sun laid rest.

The Staged Photo had the Look of a Staged Photo

Forget Kotty these avenues
the obelisk vista hold still
a smashed neo lib can you cry
a bit with your sister? That's it
razor and tape now orange,
justice together and kiss her.

I said I'd stay until the weather breaks
and then under the linden
a drizzling postcard in time
to move out of the summer

extension, in the dust of a doorway
trains churning overhead links
who was it, smiling at you on the floor
auburn or the bear

and his dogs all over damp late
summer noses in the crook of my neck
tender at Schönhauser Allee rendezvous
where are you don't be late

badly wanting the black jumpsuit
platonic cuddles for humans.

Coronelles Set 1

(2020)

to Dolly, Myra, and Phil

*Cesspits are usually buried underground, so won't take up
room on your property—apart from one manhole
which is needed for access.*

*I danced on a Friday
When the sky turned black
It's hard to dance
With the devil on your back.*

A sum... flung yearly into the cesspit of this single vice!

*At a deeper level, though, what seems most fascinating
about the state's response is the way in which it has been
performed, via the media, as a sort of melodramatic dress
rehearsal for the full mobilization of domestic
counterinsurgency.*

I AM A FREE
I AM NOT MAN
A NUMBER

1.

White seething hot glamour commons yesteryear.
I danced in the morning through the flowers
and the ash, yielding not to demi-plié, to
sting away the day oh, National Servant, say! I danced
in the morning when the trees
caught fire I punched out my eyes
in the clear well waters.
I stooped to the floor and I let my blood,
loved before the dawn of time put on some slap
karat out
I'll stand with arms high
and heart abandoned no-comply kiki
like risible kings to the dawns of a haven't summer.

2.

Stare down into the pond. It stings a bit giddy
up it's time for you ever lovely heart again to drum
oh be my ionised ballast. Tree to flame bit off more
giddy up my bravest J, you're not behind me
                    in the kitchen
a ghost went by my back
                    said a long protracted sound
against the neck, for I am just now too tired to speak
to you loved you in split up forceful right
get out
                    there in the garden of teats
my heavy load, surfacing goodbye Mr.
laughing intels, them too cringe long back across the morning.

3.

So in my tallest maxi dress / hotline goes dead,
come again to the beach my babe. I danced in the morning
and never more was said, no one was dead:
I *danced* the ionised no-comply gristle these sands away / a-boating
　　　　　　　must there fighting bit retain
take down my details:
　　　　　　　Not consent. Not. No
sarongs no shirt no entry, so I *danced* in the flowers
for the world once again agape I am ready
to dispatch:
　　　　　　　My perfect, spotless Righteousness
The great unchangeable *I AM* motherland sorrow.
There, down in the little pool where deer go to drink.

4.

NUCLEAR DISARMAMENT! Snog the mouth
under the trellis bellowed piers unyielding honeysuckle,
Dungeness scarecrow. Hello I'd like to speak to your
ruinous non so different head, *hello* this is trailing beach light danced
                staccato nebula; pause. A grating instinct
hammers in, the lights of the shore a-sway
            the utter law of the land.
Swing out a little karat, little skiff ulterior, sure
line up the flock back they go to school again the peaceful little lesion.
Time to go!
                There's a mirror showing me the ugly truth.
These bones they ache with holy fire. Jolie bruine, moon and
moon this night I creep away my love insisting on.

5.

Goodnight. If you have to go to the bathroom, just knock.
May I reach across the city. Weary unimagine.
I knocked on the graves I did the things moths did, glimpsed
and retreated *to be remembered with pity* the larvae
                feed on dry matter
not I match make ait to sob for pleasure
                stupid agape at you
air cut angle balcony you and I flung off your nut
coated like the moon's agonised east-west parade
victory agog. What is the soaking air for
                greater things have yet to come
and greater things are still to be done in this city 856,500
new faces peering in at the rancid management gateway.

6.

Where no horse should there be I danced like a sack
of shit, increased fibre optic reach, DID 9/11,
wrote a think piece; no one knows he's in the sky the ecstatic
humours rose: I danced in the servatives I danced
               in the self I planned
demi-plié to a sassy épaulement
                 negatyues
not consenting to live a giddy life by the land
by the law made up
for heady scratchings
                 we stand tall!
No turning back we found our way my immortal blind
summer unfrost cycle blathering spigot, we stood tall.

7.

The game's afoot! Like fuck I danced
nobody saw me you can't prove a thing,
are you detaining me?
Am I being detained?
              Oh Lord, I was so cherished
in summer playing arrest like a big clammy pup
            my amnesty
rests on nothing, jealous white glamour
catch me, catch me! Oh, let me dance
on imagined hooks
              perfect and blameless life
given as sacrifice one step closer, kiss me
your puppet trussed in tawse, the supreme double negative.

8.

What freedom is? I longed to glide across the floor.
Nymphette sit to pop in the morning
garden, mock targets on the swain: caloric
brain stabbers, wretched bunglers.
                        June comes spilling in.
Not enough bandwidth
                        chattering blue tits
knots of butterflies wired to the scrambled moon
steady now cut out my groaning mouth
love comes pnictogen hydride
                        who would true valour see
let him come hither concrete angel chop
suey, rally to what most are un-allowed; what each one won freedoms is;

9.

Job centre interviews on cosh, journal entr-
ists, militant democrats, slideshow glides honest
eons ago I knew you from a dream my elder
sister stay those, leg stay here pour across
                    the ground with me boss-
man, how to go on love you for the private heart to sing loud
                    crushed up alive you go
down to thorax wall I blister love really you do all the greatest
nowhere left to go perhaps I pirouette in steam,
the limit of pain and suffering is what one you endures,
                    the breezes and the sunshine
and soft refreshing rain every little thing, burn
the watered air from where you dream.

10.

Everything circles the carpet. Drive away,
stay with all torn off yer head
pulley this sicko LARP, you read:
"as is to be expected, such clampdowns
                always also backfire.
Counterinsurgency is, after all,
                a desperate sort of war
conducted only when more robust forms of conquest,
appeasement and economic incorporation
have become impossible."
                When the sky was starless
in the void of the night give it up: Somebody else's world
goes bang the birds in the air, the falling *bang* the irradiate kiddies.

11.

For the sake of the element the verse destroyed
ripped from under my failing
thinking put on the furnace again:
"The disease is often presented as if it were
                            something like a natural
disaster—at best random,
                            at worst blamed on the "unclean"
cultural practices of the forest-dwelling poor"
stay with me forever close that flap
or the sky gets in
                            that I speak no more
and my bowels be set in aspic without walls. Mundane voyage
out to the lonesome heart pathetic and strewn on the fence.

12.

Of course we're torn apart
tuned up to explode or buckle
the heat of the day the strangled mind
I saw you walk through the flies
                    and doggerel
cameras twitching
                    bad bad
weird. I wondered the possibility
they'd follow you forever like crows
to crucified bodies in hell, that
                    strongholds come tumbling down
a banner that flies across Islington, negative approach, parasites;
I think of your ashes today, if they should rest awhile on us.

13.

Please try not to spread yourself
don't be so *crying*, take my gaberdine.
You're listing in the swell.
A day of barely pressure
                sticky soft fire
permeable char-haze
                why so dam-
age don't be so *blistering*
fat on nectar, follow me says wanked up
daylight flies a sticky bun
                there's a way we can go there
we can live there beyond time 9 crimes low almost
everything I do, I do for fear of you.... *EAT!*

14.

Dressed as a fish he
waddles amongst us.
"The Mayor! The Mayor!"
cried the succulent clubs,
          but over the fields the pressure hive
a danger sought to doctor you.
          The bandits are raw,
the sea stars no more:
Come ye poindexters! Dingbats!
Ron English's whitewashed a pike!
          'Cause I can see what
the devil's trying to take now, may it be astra et luna;
proceed to the checkpoint and get to fuck.

15.

In the very beautiful dusk we spoke about the bins,
(our burnished tongues of bronze),
This is littering. If you can take a plastic bag
full of bottles into the park, you can take it out with you afterwards,
and dispose of its contents yourself
in a responsible manner.
Currently, the data shows that the R value
for England stands at 0.75. The total annual repayment cost
of all PFI schemes and repayments will be (at least) £9bn a year
for the decade. Oh good.
Your grace has found me just as I am
empty-handed but alive in your prize braun, forget about clearing,
naughty boys get sent outside. Now go on, get back to the rats.

16.

Spider crawling up your spine; across the dunes
the King of the Tussocks, sheer blanket dawn
furies through the night;
just before the fucking "sun" came up
                    we saw Dunblobbin.
gleaming through the trees.
                    28km from Foxton.
Magnitude 5.6. Look at all the piglets
who's a lovely fury? Pulling our legs off
back to the castle, oh,
                    whose voice the waters heard
and hushed their raging at Thy word. I'm back. "Good riddance",
muttered the furious king as we traced our lives back to the sand.

17.

I put on my cossie and went to your grave.
A gentle wind rocked the nettles.
The silent hole stared up to the sky.
You died in dephlogisticated air.
                    No one can deny
that these are difficult times.
                    I don't know where you're buried.
I have tried to find you,
but even so you are not there, whatever may remain,
and so breath comes in nasal compulsions. And in the dark hour
                    some thorns buried deep
and the tears that he cried as she tended his wounds. Palomino, burn
in the throes of a wretched holiday, she sang as she sewed in his hair.

18.

Very tender, ever quiet
falls away the field.
Blurring haze forget me not
the moss who holds your head.
                    The city is almost silent
sloping out to sleep,
                    the stars
who sing our closures over the earth;
the trembling morning moths
crack up to snow.
                    Your peace in our hearts
at the end of the damage. Heavy water / I'd rather be sleeping,
put out the lights of London.

19.

It's the end, but the moment has been prepared for.
Guts at dusk / the warm heart fiasco.
Pump the gear scalpel brains remoulding
zither to grate; climate neutral company;
                    cum stockade
vipers writhe in verdant
                    dust nudged past the pill.
Watcher you, devil our heart.
Strapons. Disagreements. Can 2020 just
chemical burns latest in search for missing persons
                    we do our marching to one beat
crushing the enemy under miasma, shut up bluebird
the way has been prepared for...

20.

BAMBOS CHARALAMBOUS. Crates arriving,
dockers holiday, concrete coffin,
the band venom slides its way to the front of the mouth,
pickles there. As is a router to a blind man's eye
        test weakly slides the moon
across the borrowed forest.
        The last thing we need is a seventh summer
of love, softfash avant *air*ists,
idpol variants, five year old gaffa over a drawn on mouth
LARPing round the henge. What love could mean;
        there's a cemetery deep below the sea
where I'll hide from news of the GOP. Who are parents? Jogalong
this table's taken. *Floreat Bambos*: *Labor omnia vincit*.

21.

Today I miss the poets: The Peter Manson cactus
garden, the Frances Kruk cobweb
dispensary; going into London flying out our hands:
The wholesome queer ultraviolence Rahaline vertical assault.
          A tortoise far below
skirted in rain / switched your lungs back on and then went still.
          Risk calculated against life
opposed to life at risk I danced, jackal, I *hardly* danced.
You can put a fly in the fridge for one minute place it on the windowsill:
Seeming dead. Rest it in your hand appearing to magic it to life. Wow.
          I danced in the moon
and the stars and the sun my heart will go on, black planet! It will!
They all go "*wow*" and clap and their hands. The hot fly floats away.

22.

If the objects in hell don't work, switch them around:
I.E. Red blooded Capricorn *for* Red Army Capybara.
For all the new soothsayers none turned a card for *this*
death turned giddy in elective vagaries
                    adaptive ecumenical counsel,
a heads up your finger won't put to cloth
                    here in constant fouetté
turns that sew the throat to avuncular data, relapse
shut up, dent, this thing's gone ripe someone saying something
about organs of the state, welded into homes
                    bitter was the night
before the break of day resistance 1. resistance 2.
Are you getting anything? Is that a pipe into the skull?

23.

Here's Noseybonk: We danced in the morning
for the sake of the young we went back to work
we lost our jobs we pled like servants
clover bloat, bone on bone. Over the hills
        methane obstetrics
pair off by chance. It's hot in the garden. The filthy
        jealous wailing
prius contesting the year: I danced in the night time
trembling in bed. You wailed about your *feelings*
Ziyang Fan, Head of Digital Trade, World Economic Forum;
        take me as you find me
all my fears and failures what are all these bands so angry about, purity
ziplines into dampers, heat in the sorrowing whip.

24.

In the first Spring we grew bold.
We asked ourselves 'who might die?'
We have to account one day
for our helplessness. I don't see the death
                    I don't,
more, I wanted to suffer, long and hard.
                    Poisoned again
intimate you piss off shreds of stagnant beef
quick scan started here cometh the dreamer:
This city turns people into shadows
                    when I stand in that place
free at last you have won the race sleeper in metropolis solitudo,
fiaba per un mistero sepolto tra verdi siepi, in preda ad un cuore che pulsa.

25.

With one tired horse denial of work, efficiency
line communication; dwindling spiral of control.
The process is long the poppies to seed
sweet as vinegar mit coconut sprawled across the sea
          who fixes the levy
staked out for the dogs
          sonorous filth be upon you.
Ardent love surrounds me like a blister pack,
I used to go to work each day eager through the dreaming coil
left my love behind me on the horse without his entrails.
          Hoof and horn, hoof and horn
all that dies shall be gunged fly by night I never met another gemini,
so with one tired horse and our packs we trudged out along the earth.

26.

I Am a FREE
I Am Not MAN
A NUMBER.
Precious seizure; dance, dance,
                    wherever you may be. There's ants
in the salad. Send it back. Bullet holes in glass
                    but you'll find the ants
give a zesty crunch. We go to the cancellation
fun run: Refused are the best band in the world. Nizlopi
are the best band in the world. Avicii on bagpipes.
                    Lord of all hopefulness
Lord of all joy, daughter of the sun I was raised
to do no harm and go down quiet. The heat screamed *'(Riot! Riot! Riot!)'*

27.

Daubed in off-brand kedgeree, my silent eyes to you,
my love, I walked home in the cancelled rain
and turned into a shadow. Every door was painted red.
The dead are in their aspic, awaiting resurrection
                    and outside some children are playing
in the square. They do not turn to shadows,
                    though they are parts of the city
and the clouds who do not come to sing;
the spider dangles by her hook the aching sea calls to the shore
who waits for the wounds to fall. Even the eyes who roam
                    all of my deeds, everything I've achieved
cannot earn my way to favour or a shoulder to the wheel, particles
fall like singing stones. Tako takoti o takoti sman yamba takoti.

28.

and I'm so glad I'm not in school, boss.
Switch the machine off, boss. I tethered my horse;
when the militia arrived I hid under a heap of sacks.
My breath was held in, tight, ever so tight,
           it will betray us all.
Stem for survival. The hegemony
           of the agonised tawse:
Endut! Hoch Hech! My Bonnie lies over the ocean
my Bonnie lies over the spooky abandoned house.
Oh, doubters! Oh, come declare your lives:
           His form was of the manliest beauty,
his heart was kind and soft transfiguration head over fist
I'm so glad I'm not in school, boss, beating away at my tedious head.

29.

Playing at pilgrimage; the problems of work;
if there is in fact a life regained, switched on
tampering with the clamp eyes thrown out the skull
glanced sunlight therapy trips inside the little ear:
    How do you make curfew
force the headrest out,
     so there all he goes
pissing in his bunker rushed in by secret
demand "I do nothing for nobody", truth inching in
liber mucous; terror in drastic actions right ahead
     running out of breath
the fight beneath your feet the humming acceptance speech
disgust that turned its stupid ear again to cracker shame.

30.

I am a free thinking anti-authoritarian, I said
to the nebuliser, I screamed at the cleaner,
I whispered to my mother as I spilled
into the world. That's obviously not what's meant
                    said the dry roasted crusty
changing the locks.
                    There's more at stake than granite!
The games a-fucking-foot, my friend!
You'll never get away with this. I'll see to it
you rot in jail. I wondered where my king had gone
                    entered our world, your glory veiled
not to be served but to serve, he is the boy, the past is a grotesque animal.
I never went back to finish it, the dead end stuck in the neck.

31.

Accomplices Not Allies: Abolishing the Ally Industrial Complex
(indigenousaction.org) realises the ally as temporary...
'Think, allies want something from you, in a moment. Strategy:
Accomplice: 'A person who helps another commit a crime'. 'You can
                    now pay hundreds of dollars to go to
esoteric institutes for an allyship certificate in anti-oppression. You can
                    go through workshops and receive an
allyship badge. In order to commodify struggle it must first be
objectified. This is exhibited in how "issues" are "framed" & "branded."
Where struggle is commodity, allyship is currency.'
                    Some chosen source as was need not be
the only pattern to build a world on. Where pathways meet, low
down the sound of law, burning horrified ones, take up your screaming.

32.

Let our spite rise in love
the new normal
fresh horrors our austerity
harder, faster,
                    with attention
to the detail
                    of the body,
tracking it through the world, closing its magnetically sealed
doors its airtight perimeters; let our spite
rise in love, in tender revenge
                    the trumpet sounds
and the dead will then be raised that terrible, terrible night: Dialogue
has never been our option, closed doors, brackets. Bodies through
                                        the world.

33.

Chew around your speaking lips.
Where are you, Jacq?
Do the plants stare blank the raining sky?
At the base of the lock I used a small light;
          the lamps at forty four
were out, I went to signal across the air.
                    Is anyone there? The little flicker
in the bottom left glass, silence. Silence in light.
Oh death where is thy sting? Angels,
moth dust,
                    that sacred pot of red stuff
could blow me out, ribbons undone, gentle joy;
if we'd only allowed for our confiscated world...

34.

Starry ribband beds about his wings
their cobbled lilies clog-danced,
on planted earth wallow'd about he stands
so we bare the shavings, and suddenly
                    the light air beating easterly
at frozen plummet front;
                    their lives would fall to bits
by auctoritee of persones
we go out to build;
a problem with the axle. Though
                    I have a sweet hope
of glory in my cold little heart. 22 letters
to the council, and *still* no arrests. The scorn of the tussling bins.

35.

Amongst the herbs & electricity. The air
rolled through the blockchain, & you were crying
again, waiting for the knot to crumble down.
A delivery of proper medicines. No food.
                    The buildings speak, unyield
beyond paraphrase. Dock your mouth.
                    The spectral spiders screech
and creak: False. They are silent, you cannot imagine
the terror in wordless descent, the never screaming
jaws, the silent armoured limbs;
                    it sounds an echo in my soul.
How can I keep from singing? Laid to rest & gathering herbs:
Eat well, exercise. Live to be devoured.

36.

Throw the yo-yo down; it comes back up.
Nothing is ulterior. Paradox is dead.
I believed in pure Justice: The difference
as striking as the common. I cannot read Our Death:
            That the pain realised themself
to struggle, the stammer of packaging. I have never cried.
            My whole life, eyes sewn shut. They beg
to leak. The world rejects. Strength, head wound, the virus.
This thing inside, it killed us: Fuck balconies. Fuck the world
reject. Reject. Reject.
            You pushed away the maelstrom.
You made us believe. Resistance 5 resistance 7
resistance 6, that the eyes be allowed to spill themselves outside
                                            in deleting air.

37.

We must go on. Through the sloping rain
and the new builds. Staring over my head
my eyes turn up through aching bone.
We climbed the lighthouse.
                    A voice echoed blank, no face
in slate ahead
                    be careful as you go
oh, please take care. There is horror deep ahead
and nowhere else to step,
it waits like a pit who circles you, take care where you will go.
                    Amante è la musica che con noi non finisce.
Strapperò le ciglia con le mani, lascerò per sempre il luogo dei
                              miei maniaci pensieri.
Yesterday once more whisper please take care, my darling one,
                    be careful where you tread.

38.

One pain stops. Knock. Wandsworth. Call out. No more
aversion therapy, to jump start new death
rippling through the trees. Ladies at court
riven and chaste I will lie at your feet.
                    Mocked in traction
bonded to air I am still breathing. Lucky
                    to be, hir ribbons at the wrist.
Knock. Stammer for reason, the chest heaves up we march again
voiceless young say their names, saints, purchased in blood
the destroyer went blind dusted off against the spoiling line.
                    Bonum est confidere in Domino,
bonum sperare in Domino spite and malice knock three times
pushed away digging out the eyes. 002023647.

39.

Now's our chance. I signalled with my lamp across the gap.
Knock. A flicker of red in a torn up corner. How can it be
so long away I wrapped myself in the curtain to signal
over the air, you are not there.
                    Knock, that now I am sleeping, the window is open.
the ladder is propped against the scaffolding, you so far gone not across
                    to air or sky gone so much,
silent of light no light in silence creaks away the forty four windows
stare. Way far back even then. Knock. It will not pass it simply doesn't
go, far enough to hear this light who shrieks across the firmament
                    plunged beneath that flood lose all
their guilty stains hewed in the brand skin and atmosphere
to a little dimming tint, be careful where your light treads soft ahead.

40.

She advances to meet the jaw, the plastic
second trapping. It waits & opens up its net.
One group. One body of organs.
An un-renounced crypsis
                    so deathish calamistrum.
Reach across the silent evening. Beg to fall to sleep.
                    A violent stridulation sucking
stomach. Resistance. Disease. Resistance. Disease.
Rejected where the lung proscribes.
All the limbs removed
                    & she goes on
without the head. Now, o now, o silencer
a speckled band appears, absence can no joy to thee impart.

41.

By the swell of the Brapple, new day at last. Scorn hangs in the tongue,
the assailing mandible, correctly infers with rain to PAT test the stutter:
Terrorism is the worst thing in the world. Ripe crops bolt upright
swell their chests to any scrambled data, perturbed to telling,
              I am dead to you.
  For God sake, *eat something, please.*
          When have you ever worked.
This is what not realising looks like. We should separate the hostile world
The whole orange air migraines into your swelling eyes. You are the furies
screaming at the camera, your children in the room above, pressed into
                                     the corners.
          Zealots fire that bigots warms,
Fury's wrath that fools alarms, Hell and misery, everyday life, goodbye,
he snarled to the begging window, old uncle Tom Cobley and all.

Coronelles Set 2

(2021)

dedicat. Alice Bradley and the Mammoth Org

final disprove

Robbery crime waves swept the world.

under avalaunch two hours found dead resuscitated came to life

you are on the case magnifier to your eye

*My horse shied... and down we both came... But I stood true vermin,
and tried the islands afterwards for snipe.*

Remember, don't be barbarous. It is bad.

NO MORE

1.

Let me breathe you in. Copper above, kitty alone.
A tipsy light is tilting through the earth.
Peel away the soil. Stare into the ground.
This window, one of forty four
                    peering back to where a tiny light
signals over the wire. The gap
                    is spoken trauma
the snarling angle to stare. Breathe the dead bacteria
fall and swell like a lung, a brain closing down.
Waiting on deliveries of medicines
                    time spreads across the dead weight of the air.
Factory settings down by rote, don't know where don't pass me by
to shake the earth. A haunted knock below the covered lid.

2.

A trill along the road.
Walking at impossible angles
dumped horizon aches
against the eye. Knots of fleas
pepper the sheets. 4.1%
choked apart cadavers
crackle numbing
twilight arks down
no sight, near
      even song.
      Gaping rave
graphic stench.
A knock the wire forbade.
     It creaks
      to the shelter,
hands cracking lips
harsh in fury step.
Fingers scattered
to a frozen floor
speaking to
something, gone.
     It would
      not answer.
Like snow down in the shelter
returning blank air, gathering
fingers in a plastic net.
The building, begin. Eject.

3.

But for you to go so far, an air insisting on.
The trees are bright asleep. A canister in the ground.
A knock of sky night felled.
Northerly or northeasterly. Knock. A sky. What is a sky is air
                so fall away. List a-sway glance knock to ever air,
across a sluicing face mote and motion hewed. Just
                past gone that air that mouth took in.
Roar apart the fuse intake to stutter the running board.
No breath across the airway. Knock. Singed gasses fed back out
deficient world, horizon: The tread familiar street. A body screams
                O, pretenders let's fall down
the past is a grotesque skyline
knocked to draining colour.

4.

Remember the Beetle Drive my chestnut?
We were dressed in ham. You won for us a goldfish.
What's the point? This private aulicism. I'll get up
tomorrow, climb into my scaly skin.
                    You are (as a spoke)
sublimating pink airs;
                    look how imminent you are. Something in forever
changes; a green seeping lamp or blue lightning flat on a disk,
the smell of it. A history bloating its chest like a spiritual
sky. You absolute show off *I love you* I asked, very weakly
                    and watched as each door swung slowly shut.
You can buy your way back, but it won't be the same. You weren't
much good anyhow, writhing with violence and crookedness. Strike out
                    my love once more across the world, and try again.

*a. In weaker sense: to give a faint or intermittent light; to shine
faintly. Also with away, out, and quasi-transitive with cognate object.*

5.

Softly drunk the amyl park distends. I am mollusc.
It is not disgusting. Something creepy
is happening. It's hard to dance now, but the detail is raw,
we must proceed, really we *have* to go on. Over the big pipe.
                    Don't cry
it's the morning
                    there is light
work ahead. A note to a friend dead mollusc. Endurance athletes.
Tiresome as hell, still, to skate beyond the dark night...
When did we speak to ask you to
                    lay down your head
for sorrow, Jo/cqui/hnny, we want to see Jesus lifted high
over the glimmering nitrate haze to the dogs in the park.

As the sonne vppon the water whanne it is Glemerynge.

6.

I brought a tongue to the meeting.
Began to backslide again.
Somewhere in the memory bank.
The motion of a celebrant.
                    I threw myself in the bin.
A finger tapping the window.
                    Emaciated
eldership speaking of commerce
waves beating at a ship in peril
lower the life
                    raft higher and
higher here is the corn. My bonnie lies over
the stuttering storm: Weather conditions deteriorate.

7.

excitable notions of liberty
faded life instilled
through hazing
passive tellings
              within the confines
of a ceremony someone revolting
              these books
conversion lurches
banished love
where the sacred
              practice instilled in the nerve
all glimpses a new world flattened
if symptoms persist apply rank cough punish

8.

Voices like static in a universe
I can't get through. My hands activate.
The phone dies. The rescue beacon mimicked light
along the stern
                    compressed air filling
the life raft. Emerald
                    broke down
in the reef bed,
two white bones, a third
puncture
                    you could take
the world week in week / *and out* / all these rivers.
Do you read? Send help (the beacon, its failure to function).

9.

I'm better now, and time spreads away
across the flood. If you hate flying ant day
we hate you. I was having flying ant
day dreams in the flying ant
            daycare flying ant-
ibiotics to the depots over the millions
            of grasses back along
the unyielding year before the drunken morning
blustered in, spoiled against the shine. Sapphqui
stares up through swinging emerald drops
            you were singing over
me four green fields, flying ants, a fleet
of deans, the little splitting waves cut off the blood.

10.

To stand
outside a door
the pressure
the world entirely
& forever
that fearsome life
itself, too much
bared, scrapes
the dust deep in wire wrap
                squashes
                    the spider's body
brown-grey
pouring pustule.
                    Sometimes
                made to stand
to bare outside a closed door.
In the barriers, in locking
in the small breaks cresting
the waves in the narrow
between building & sky.
Up and down the balance
                of the
                tide-measure,
in the brink of the air
in the eye in
the pickle jar,
the spider's locking hairs. Protecting empty space.

11.

There's harm simmers in the street
chews the root. These faces: Each
cries out to left to right a lost name
coiled in bandage. A collapsed nest dangles
in the sea. The thought will not test you
take you inside. The bodies and faces
they lurch and plank
a needle & hacksaw a tedious moan
that is the landscape this foul colloidal heart-
beat. Restricted access. Protected.
Do you look at the moon my little
loon? // Resistance 1. Resistance 1.
Those that are vocal. Those who are made to kill.

12.

Cruelty, cruelty! *Tomorrow*
we ride and history itself shall bend
to my ribbons & heart your millions of air:
Volcanoes erupt, the ground
trembles and molten lava spews
forth from inside the earth.
The trees are quiet.
The birds whisper jasmine
              soft rain
              trimmed to perspex.
Everybody loves trains,
from the huffing
                   puffing whistling
                   steam impact report align
the connection support (acc. no. 9313), Jackee, you plank!
...and fix it against the wall. Angular momentum, desiccated
kidneys. Iron. Our splitting,
seas coming to rest like radio
splutter. The second apex
              blown to and fro.
              In case your plan falls
through to
mispronounce my name,
orange spider
muted mourning:
The day
is down
              so come, my
              daughters, sting!

13.

The year to be alive too sharply snapped.
I saw the dead. I danced in the morning
poured out my lungs,
light vanishing under the door.
                    All of the care that entered
fresh at first afraid
                    swelling in the afternoon
with Jacq, on the grass. *Glooms so,*
they bellowed in the air: Indifferent pressure
there is harm in this order that stutters and shines:
                    What a few reactive pressures
do to the wires: Spit. Prosthetics. Resurrection, & back
through the pouring sky the year itself to be swallowed.

14.

Hammers. Entrepreneurs. Moth dust.
Oh sick bright summer glitter
through the roof. Extract the face.
Calm yeast settles in. Fungal powder.
                    Oh I wish to set you to freedom
Jacqui, if only I could speak some new arrangement
                    the face over my left shoulder
there, all the time, in a constant strain to speak
to you again as I am now as you were and he was
there Jacq are you there come out of the cupboard
                    a bear met Algie
that's where I shall be so shaking on the sand who is this
that engulfing kindness eyes search after, nor to see again.

15.

How do I deal with this talking head on its spike?
I've seen this kind of mouth before.
The car park is full of bones. She's up to her waist in creosote,
and so on, through the mire. Pressure pads.
                    The bones smell so sweet, abolished,
the sound of air expelled from peat. It is securely chained up in there.
                                                        In you go.
                Count the windows again. Forty four or so
despicable acts treatment, the *sheer angle* of the thing!
Here we stand in the cold and the sleet
it is early and bitter a little pool to wash your feet in, 1992, something
                idiotic to clutch at like a piping ball of ham
festering on Threadneedle street, ice falling onto the shoulders,
                    poltergeists, wasps, headshots, spoiled water,
that strange pressure in your forehead loosed in gorgeous pink,
                        green, blue, plasma, fibre optic lights,
the door is ajar, don't look back & (joy shall be yours in the morning).

16.

Stop. Going back late over the shoulder on the tiled floor
hot body compress on cold bulging out the swimming giant
eyes on fire rip to twitch finding out praying
for aspic covered. Body. Aspic covered hot dead heart machine
                        in favour
into the city. Find out the cupboard get in there Jac
                        he's come for me hot greased body bathroom floor
sink unit, shower basin, grout, test. Break isolate
tor swing out giddy
spilling siren not condense
                        I danced in the
morning follows me like greased light floor
show droughted music closing terrible down in light.

17.

I walked alone with your pieces
into the park.
Our hands touched
two butterflies swirled into the air.
The horizon triangulated
as our tiny hearts
witnessed the stretching
tide collapsing. The failing dream world to paste.
                                        Leave now.
                    It had to end so we
                    turned
to the grass.
Laid out in dappled light
                    a ribbon wrapped
                    around our sleeping arms.
We washed the leaves,
stared into the sky.
There was nothing left
nothing at all. Even the finished sky finished breathing
                                        water. It is what
it has meant to be evaporated.
Taken kindly into a new world;
                    to run
                    through asbestos
run, first and last for you, dear lost Jack,
this tiny murmur creaking
in the branches. No need
to come back for here again at last.

18.

When I was but thirteen
or so I was already gone away,
and the scaffolders
like a tool in a day
or sobered to uncertain points
of a single word
in a world
                    are not
                    the only recourse
in a day of life just as the world
is a cesspit of a tool
                    and I was being told
                    that it is not defined by a person
or a girl who was a huge part
in a world of a single clamp
in a day and a time
so as I would love to the people of God
who is a CLOSED noise
who has a most powerful witch
                    and a few years before you arrived
                    A tear,
Sarah Jane? No,
don't cry.
While there's
life there's…

19.

But what of this sun
this air these long
toothless days
the stammering face
of the water, who cares?
Primed to explode quietly the edict
to the tongue the sinus passageway
roars in extremis. Stair gate after lock
             the standby
             flickers
dust
kicks up
             glass scratched
             eye grid slimmed
to breaking. Choice
we sang to steer away
the freezing harbour
clutched inside the rebel heads
asway tinned fish tender supple
lighting what more
             a good command
             of vibrato
is all that is required; how can I keep
from singing my last
breath invisible pours into the summer sky
awake and gently gumming.

20.

Dry as court peripheral fear to piss be seen
police unguarded local bolt doggerel,
and so the promise lock ahead for better children, come, for
posh natural grand summer spread amongst the pastel
                    frocks to perfect dirt or grass
stained knees untented humans
                    miles across the sea, not you.
Oh better lock with hateful eye that hate is made to shut up
sieve out the needles, summon in constables, Cllr Phélim
fury beaten panic skin dried off the draft comes down and
                    so we spoke and so he spoke lock it up the square
eyed pack hampers back to gentle earthly
lovely call the powers down to scrub the bodies out.

21.

Porcine gentling. Rigorous scrimshaw. Fashionable housing.
Pamphlets like jockeys: small, moneyed, short lived.
Couldn't dream a more scrupulous niche
doing the cryptic pedal to the floor
                fold back into reaching air.
I ate a tin.
                It felt meals.
There is a weeping you
stabbing into the chest
its little guilts I file away the letters in my gut, stare across the field.
                Don't look back
cos they're not waving. The animals were gone. The call
comes through, a tangling sound in the head and neck. Night mit
                                dear worry.

22.

Vat grown skin flickered to brackish currents.
The *Immortal* commands it, creeps there, struck.
All the trees are dead. Look at the dead trees.
Look at you crumpled pieces what is it that
                          trees dead
extract
                          you say
there is a city
is no
street beyond there is no air
                          no blast furnace light up
the sky with standard face: Face down again
split trees gnashing. Without fire without air total separation.

23.

The moon is hobbling
round the wall.
The hero
devotes. Shakuntali
        Siberia a chucked out sea
inside a wall, spite
        itself
punched through. A fistful
of sea
hurtles apart
        by the moon
disgusted to see
this morning you afraid.

24.

Kratom
beyond scorched blood
the churning night
that you were still alive
            our boiling cells
too bright
            gloom it takes to hear
your voice again: Very silent
closing my eyes to concentrate that life
you disappear
            or find you here
with ease. So much so you come again and again
to the world, local ever as night.

25.

Bromide, at last. We pressed our feet together.
Please let's build *something*? Some kind of tubular
lining? Everything is falling to sleep again,
or rather there is no sleep, just closed eyes and trembling.
             I danced down the topsoil
rat-juice in tulle stood like a fracture
              A - on stolen time as in lampreys
A - is no sleep in this coffin its landscapes & corrective
therapies its herd notions there is not a people who are us
but rather that we have spilled and our juices
              are poisons are set to bleach the ground one face:
Mine. It appears at the window all stupid and ghostly
I have ratified your structure but finding out meant absolutely nothing.

26.

Acute variance—soil pressure—
& fading skies. Beholden
at stress your body map leaking
torn to peppered in scab
the days they close you 1 by
1 in torn up heads like
batter & bay & scorn so deep in love
scattered like hands data in ribbons
       undelt like an air-wound;
mirrors at pressure deep in the earth
electricity. Let me breathe you
       unfelt like a haunting
is gone like a life
a young body torn
about in electric rise deft & I
both are scathing hewed
in a breach of the heaven's laughing
bodies are let there to rot
       buildings unfeeling
26. To weld the people into
one loving unbreathable sky—this
is our sagging confessions in love—
be utterly changed into fire.

27.

Then, BEAT neurotic sky sore
happy little friends.
O mild lovers mask
to tweezer out the gutter
      sour slipping
liquid voices shield
      its wrenching tenancy
corrupted faces in the stones
its cacophony: A dusk: A
beating: A *feeling* line
      O, pretenders
let's go down shine on blast
pretends itself a feeling.

28.

The autumn tides. Nothing.
Mute me. Good god, the nothing.
How much? Nothing, nowhere
on. They go up. Changes. Something
                    happens next
nothing. Up and away. The nothing
                    happens each day
no, how. It goes. It all away
goes nothing happens mute. I am
on nothing mute by the autumn tides
nothing event
                    comes away my
nothing's what. Comes away
good god the nothing happens tides away.

29.

Cranes mimic the flickering sky.
The greater sacrifice
the sea
poisoned body
           beating the door
with its fists
           seven strokes
terror. Look into
my eyes. My eyes is
the door is deprogrammed
           beating out
your eyes, heart, capacity,
eight eons nothing ventured.

30.

Comes away to static. Die in dot of eye
formed to leak
investigate
shut. No driven mean. Survive.
            Damp falls up
screwed into grill
            the flat one the paste
drum. They lay strapped to the nose.
I was feeling like there is a thick plate
pressuring my chest and also needles
            poking my chest
spite spills into a spoilt pillory: Fuck it
let them paste and fall *spin and fall* shut them.

31.

Beware of your conditions.
i. *Do not be the enemy.*
Say nothing. *You will carry*
a sign. Be marked
with double tongue. ii.
Strength. Swallow it.
Like the fire you are
become loosen the clamp.
      iii. It will gulp
      your minds,
your materials *and spirits.*
They will tear out this building
      its heart
      and poltergeist.
Another lifeless tree. Look at it.
Note it. Hold it in your brain.
iv. *For contumacious desire*
destroys its owner,
makes her the sport
of her enemies.
      xxviii. Happy in my
      agitate. Flowers snap to
cobalt *in the* bloodstream. xxix.
Fear *lights the way*
to the beautiful prow. It is morning.
Dread appears and *sings* itself like breath.

32.

One day, maybe not a day there will be
no more treasure. Comb the ground for metal.
Siphon the mud. There is treasure
each day accumulates behind,
                    objects stack
inside the earth, stupid ones,
                    perfect ones,
dented ones, round ones, but one day
they will stop coming into the world
and for moments hence just bones
                    nobody
to find and name them give yourself up
for there is still the hope it cheats on you today.

33.

You have always lived here
with your name collapsed
& stayed unspread.
Clutching at
                    the podium
in someone melting's
                    bedroom
the rasping parent
shaking in the cubicle
nextdoor, *longing* to drive you back
                    to life, to quit
a while the radio which barely kisses tokens
of the law. The silent floor in sleeping blank.

34.

You danced a tiny dance. It was the fault of the bulb
its seething flicker its cell. And a frost had formed on your lips
in adverse reaction the medicines dripped feet the whole of the chest
lit up crumpled and we were screaming through the fields
   pollen hissed Hannah sing come back
awake. All of many hours cut in tongue and cell
   split away your skulls. Night falls. Gethsemane
again... Spirits hoist a gory flag the AGM-84H grins past the post
I can see a brand new epoch porous full of dead crusade into the great
wide world torn for greater promise:
   Take the adventure, heed the call, now ere the irrevocable
moment passes! 'Tis but a banging of the door behind you, a blithesome
step forward, and you are out of the old life and into the new!

35.

If life forms stutter
that you break for
gone to bits to core
or muzzled to the hinge
      it all but hovers
into air like flies.
      To see a body
melt away. A fake one
with no skin
its forearms
      hold you
like a baby, an elastic toy
to lift your breath away.

36.

Into the square
by the gallery
for the doctors,
all three of them
           annunciating life.
Pulling out a tooth
           to crayon out
the isotope
to track the limits
of one corpse
           legs above
my head
inside the ice.

37.

My perimeter. Thank God for that.
(I am fond of it). There is a crack in it.
We've got a light switch
which we use in the evenings,
          light in some circumstances, I thought
my chain link fence.
          It keeps the neighbours at a distance.
Although I do sometimes pass the time
of day speaking with them near it.
And that's the beauty of a perimeter
          over a 6 inch wall: You can see through it.
I will write a note informing you
of the problem. Thank God for that. I am fond of it.

38.

You can get lead. We had it. We used it
in the garden on the path
going through the grass. It is Monday.
You can get brushes and clocks
                    for not too much. People are going
to work
                    on the bus there are three other people
I saw a couple PCSO's patrolling the city today
buses have been running quite well lately. Here is my pebbledash
wall. It keeps my house from falling down.
                    You can walk there on your own.
I'd like to purchase a fluid. It has been getting colder.
The windows need to be closed. 14:35.

39.

The purpose in purchasing a fan is to reduce damp.
Ideally it will be easy, low maintenance, reliable
and wipe-clean. There are various shops that sell filters.
The bins will be collected.
                    I'm going to get something to eat
before I go. A picture of Montreal Road
                    from the roundabout.
The post's been.
Relieved to inform you that traffic is moving as usual.
I like playing music but my hi fi is in the shop for repairs.
                    Sunset at 8:39 pm.
Everyone socially distanced on my bus.
The parking spaces are suited to vehicles.

40.

Now it is evening, the end of the world again. There are
40,000,000 stars shining down on our cold stiff bodies.
We stare up at the stars. Dis-
gusting.
                    We look down at our hands.
The sky has failed, as has all of the air. We go to vote on the starlight.
              Everything without motion. And so today we will sleep
                            again with no bed.
We will go into the pale world and cancel the remnants of our throats.
              There is no replacement. Everything came true.
                            The light on mute
              access soft, spreading over your borrowed face.
You leave them your tongue as a present and exit the corrugate hall.
Nobody tried to call after you but there was a strange hissing
as you glided through the city. Everywhere new barriers
                    served notice it is like a dull paste this sky
that echoes onto the water. The tides. The tiny body. Nothing.
These are your feelings. This the corroded likeness.

41.

In the evening I was murdered. I went out
into the air walked towards the sea
then back towards the air over the falling leaves.
I was murdered.
        I think about the people who vanish
from the world
        those that do not simply stop living
but who claim to never have been.
Who are you, Jacq? My eyes were pouring out
across the park and I could see the whole of the world
        bleeding on the floor determined to live
for what you gave it is senseless, beautiful,
murderous year by year and for life.

42.

In the very last corner of the universe,
a cluster of sex people. It is very tiny.
A huge dog is laughing. Its comforting hands.
Your heart is going like a pressure cooker.
        There are twelve skeletons
under the floorboards. And in the last corner
        of the universe
a tiny voice is calling to you, in the woods
where the birds fell silent you were followed
through the groaning trees
        and the corner is closing in,
lift me out of the cupboard, won't you Jacq?
All that liquid tugging at the sky.

43.

This is the world. I have decided to eject the sea.
It keeps chucking itself up
onto the land and I am sick. This is the voice
of the entire world throwing the sea through the sky.
        Don't let me work alone,
next time you're near take a handful of sea and hurl it to the heavens
        scream something stupid, insistent, vengeful,
plaintive against gravity, something oh so pretty,
punch that little piece of ocean in your fist through the sky.
Nothing happens. The wind tears you up. You speak to a friend.
        Nothing comes of it. She has been silent for years.
               -     Every time you speak,
silence, both of you, nothing to come and nothing to make.
Still, you have gone down to the sea you have taken up some water
        in your fist, shown some willingness,
        now you may channel the wind. Eat.

44.

The sex people coughed in their knot. Jacq didn't take my hand.
We didn't walk away along the line of pylons. I asked her how to spell
                                                              her name
which, until our very last day together I hadn't known. I didn't weep
as we parted. No envoi. No tiny corner. I barely thought of her
                    until the need for kindness had raged in my stomach,
all kinds of violent symptoms, invoked so much shame.
                    We didn't meet at a reunion. We didn't get in touch
years later, get drunk on an empty beach, stare up at that hole
punched in the sky. Instead we went about our lives and we became
whatever we are silent to with perhaps the imprint of names, or even
                                                              forgotten forever.
...
Staring southwesterly the air catches fire, glides down into an infinite
                                                    red chaetomium weave.
May I sing to you? From very far away, and that nothing would
          disturb your waking or your sleep, but that something
     of my gratitude would find your life, or an echo of your
          world if it is over, and sing for you a skyline.

45.

Niz, if you want to slaughter Butane Lilith, tell hir ze can't
assemble in groups, then send hir back to work. There is none.
Send hir anywhere. Close the
doors. Restore factory settings.
Yearn to downplay graft tomorrow. A member of the family
Sparassidae whose bungaroosh nests require a 15% uplift
on the premium. These frozen acetates,
those darkened shops from the early 2000s with ultra violet lights and
plasma in low pink. Sunday becomes gay.
Riots cease to move. Polite home invasions by forty armed officers.
Crumbs anew get tossed them down / will some of you come back.
A gray mouth groans apart to breathe a sound:
This will be the year for great promise. I need you to
come back together. Your spirits. Bury the dead.
Move on through the air, through the park, see
the butterflies explode like squeezed food into
the throbbing dawn.
The treatment won't take long and if it hurts just press here. The wires
will come alive, shallow fry your little brains. The tides have stopped
moving. I stared for days and days at the water in
the harbour. It didn't move. As if the entire world
had resigned into some terrible rupture where every
motion stood still, the water, lying there staring up
at the blank gray sky, my mouth hanging open,
breathing without a voice.
Our love for each other let it never incinerate like one plastic cup.

46.

Are we home again, Jacky?

We mustn't stir the silt,

but I dreamed we were searching for a body
by the shores of a huge lake, divers in
            broken commlink

the dark blue sky
            woke us. We looked into one another's faces

bobbing near

to the shoreline, seconds ago.

We are nearing the datum point, Jacky,

            just by that rock

the dogs are pointing into the lake...

Postcards from Lopud

(2011)

for Rose

The finger drops, straddle quiet, very stung
a little like a dream from reached folds full
      open to rain
      baited saint, capture a polished neck.
Raised, mould and claim
as wayward. Accumulate repair. Shrines open to water,
slack chrome do rely, back to longing pitch. The saints
      suffer, a long warm shift
candles bite uncommon, scratched at the foot:
Voices pointing, receding, a little pain sloped
      the breath we're in.

A finger drops rigid, as if to clip
the neck hole straddles, careful,
mountains born
          sweat dent. Slack teeth
a vein pops to breed, ever so clear, a little
like altitude taught, why not, how best to sing?
Watch the water, know the periphery, how love
is just against it. Ask back to longing.

Wild and uncommon
bleeding ripe trust
    keen to empty in a heaped limb.
  Cracks blaze to sleep.
How silently and sweet
     some mirage to precinct thirst. Matters
  but scattered.
Glad to indicate
    knees giddied that drip
their blood to bed.
      A paddle, recognition blows
upset the lake's week sanctioned
bleated spine. Proverbs matched
    a slide, of those the heart to bite.

There was the rotten saint, there
at rested tick neural bark adonis
blue wasted clipping breath
further, a small boat dropped

pearly fingers forged, a real chest.
All the earth's nervous lilt calling to
the air, swift. People must sleep in
too benign. Hardly walking on

        peppered down
it can hurt, but you, ghostly inlet
the saint glass of your feet
and pull some breath.

There, rust among some hills,
the crutches, nails caught to a cap, the whole earth,
some skin.
                    Limits love chased the nails
                    and this microcosmic charge
          dangling from the eye, decline at the instep.
     Dotted by the well to canister waste legs.
You, lipped, gold at a thing.

Saints drip teeth in a well.
     Induced to window spill
       split tense from heads, crack out
excess of heart, tract. Chin tense,
the brow. Be extreme laughter
     octopus blink. Burn whole, unquenchable felicity.
Works entire live to habit.
     To a warm mole the hills flirt
at envy drift face first, catch me
     in try-out bait mere.
     From a comfy chair
    prosthetic wing of lime.

Songs of the Morning

(2023)

In memory of Sean Bonney.
Rest in peace and power.

1.

It's murder to hear
it won't ignite
the bricks in the structure
forego combustion

if I don't know
if I am not sleeping
if nobody is

sleeping time is being

neither dead nor fallen
black holes in our hearts.

2.

Hey, hallelujah! You're here
at last! And I saw his hand
in the garden, hospital

pale and gesturing
out to the sky

be still forever I cut
the string that makes
the hammer strike

open the lock I see
me I'm stiff with fear

3.

speak then for sleep
stays away. No one sleeps.
Whether rejecting all of pain
stuffing up the ears

getting out of your head
whatever
the exit
every part
is in active and wakeful response, still
the sun is lovely
fruitless error.

4.

Two officers are here
you are not

pain in procession
bitter aching tears necking
on the third rail

going to a torn out house
ankle deep in rain
the world you cut

as flurries in the face

calm as softest snow
the night train home.

5.

It's quiet down here
in the sky, offered up we were
dance love electrocutes
hearts awake
but a thousand days
and spirits
of descent
artlessly explode
each one left behind
is a warrant
Kodak threnody
squid ink forensic
& spattered with remains
left out to die.

6.

Types of disinfectant
intruding on grief notes
I don't see you anymore
refuse to sleep
refuse to turn away
I hope I will never feel
love for your undercut
power the wages are
sick pay slow motion drone
footage car park
memoriam. Safety
scissors, bag
of invisible gasses.

7.

My cruelest opinion
is so entertaining
dogs snap at the wheels
strollers charging

insane after business
babies paraded
in the park before work
a small heap of coins

he never could find
rent and fresh cloth
this fetish my memories
love has never turned aside.

8.

Block it. No simile
love has never turned aside
the blade, boots or bullets
neither has it ever
satisfied my hunger
of body or mind. Block.
The author of my hunger,
the architect of my circumstantial
unquiet thoughts
your civil slaughter stint;
it was Tom's hand reaching out
to each a different world.
I'll seal them up. I hope I never will
feel love for the thing that causes
insufferable pain:
That bears my name.

9.

Can she excuse my wrongs?
Shall I call her good?
I live in shit, the moon
our precious breath
it rises
over all the valleys and the sea
grins frozen
to the head
abolished the concept
of the lightweight
and pessimism, optimism
are bullshitting
mourning here to pressure
on the soil.

10.

Today, found some love here
in a major lift

agitates
the battery

our comprehending
flowers
sewn in plaits
the hair, it's complex
entity rational as well as
it is living.

11.

A hole in the sky cleared
for daylight & departure
a problem is leading the way
we must get behind
The Leader the
cyber mask is slipping
dog his trail
to infinity
for those that are disallowed
to breathe,
to pastors, criminals and even druids,
spooks and those insipid gurus and
snowstorms my hexes on the pit-mouthed
fool who thinks
that art is heaven.

12.

Today

I did not
wake up

I was not asleep

awake and fully active

in all that I was

a little end to punishment

is the uncharged confession.

13.

It will not stop: The throat
conducts the mouth, I've got
a woke, when all the time
is excused by a false sleep
but consider this picture:
Your dreams. They're loud, fantastic,
filled up with beauty
and dreadful power
just as soon they melt
of opals in the sky
GOD, GOD!
DON'T MAKE EVERYTHING
RIDICULOUS.

14.

learning to act
outside of the corner
exiled forever yet he woke
memories devoured
by beauty though nights
are dark enough
for those that are in despair
to breathe when there is no air
from the highest spire
of contentment
I thought you strong,
it is a whole.
It always was a whole
must smash the vase this
bath of trivial air.

15.

There was no other way
to think these thoughts
winged with hopes
magnetic and divine
whispers softly in my ears
my ridiculous ears
distortions of a world
remain the same distance
sweeter
blackouts
ahead

16.

Nearing the end
a compulsive
block it
silicones the gaps
black mold
and toadstools
rock the heart to fuck
this gorgeous garden
private vernacular
desperate to exit
the train glides on
it is reason's will
that stole my soul away...

...and still would not
catch fire.

17.

I live and die in thee
let's live // love
where the sun is
strange

the officers gone
from the doorway
still
you know

they're out there
stinging the floor
like a pair
of glitching medics.

18.

Block so now
we must
move forward
or I sleep and am
as vague as mist

in the gallery
clearing
high under
the moon

a mourning so
unsafe
it begins to be
beauty who sashays
and skips.

19.

The
words
are in
disconnection

unchecked—Block.

At the side
of the earth

a starling
spoke
with the voice
of a Lord.

Sean Bonney, *Baudelaire in English*
Sean Bonney, *Notes on Militant Poetics*
Diane Di Prima, *Revolutionary Letters*
John Downland, *First Booke of Songes or Ayres*
Second Booke of Songes
George Jackson, *Soledad Brother*
Tom Raworth, *Hands (January to September)*
Cat Vincent, *1000 Days*

Lollygagging

(2023)

Right to work

Heart swell's secret history
took me to the counter, considering
my mental health and trainers, affirmations
in the ear's eugenic by the deep I measured
the centre: Clever thoughts on institutions
weeks on end down from the neck failing
to report for work; it will not resolve to shame.
We'd traipse along the dyke picking samphire
                deep down in the nerve
ending echoes of You, beaten till the skin
cracked up porcine, passed around for money
truly invaded, crying, by charity and packed off
until the dormitory windows
opened like cushioned exits to deference.
New Guardians, reaching along the aisle
to my sister, not touching, we will form a cast
                I could manage the stage lights
memorise participation sending flowers
down the river. A particular smell I thought
of huge umbrella leaves floral full
cow parsley and playing at fishing enriched
danger along the protected gangway
then what do we think? A white body rises,
falls reclining in the riverbed remnants
                of a plaid shirt bursting belly
bubble breath in vomit insects
refuse of the body script:
Don't speak, new powers act to draw the aqualung
upsurge plenty abased plunged and she drew breath
as her head deep down inside would split its blood

over the furrows. My sister secured work in Limerick.
You do not speak for them, but she had to let you hear
                    producing a potent sativa
high in THC with a tenant chained to the couch
sharing the bypassed meter freelance
and I'd been wanting to get into this kind of work
myself, I could do it I know I could or they're going
to lock my cousins into the oven
a tiny hot box you can hear that,
you can hear them, banging on the roof
                    engine spluttering up
monoxide scentless or senseless we said later
museum beetles chewing at the moths
by, who knows, William Boothe a butterfly
shot down from the sky
its tattered broken binbags pinned out christ
you can hear that. can't you? Sniffing the bubble
when someone gets machine gunned
                    in a riptide very still, tender,
I think we should move on, further
the venture: At the point of death a flood
of DMT fills up the eyes in a sense, the end,
very nice, we could start a weekend retreat
together now Dover southwesterly 5
to 7 occasionally gale 8 at first in west
very rough occasionally
                    christ that's blood on the lobe
occasionally rough in far east hemispheres
thundery fruitfly micromoth full destroyer
pinned out. Preferred, with skins hosed down
plaid shirts unwashed if that child would have
no contact. You can hear that. Held
much betrayed across her distance,

passage thrive by the window
　　　　　the willows plunged and sang
faltered on a breaking tenor
the river dreaming. She was asleep.
Somebody was pounding on the door.
Peeling vegetables in the office, they'll be
along soon from the secret dormitory, you hear?
My heart dreamlike swells Derwent's Mill
　　　　　evergreen though conceited
immortality, surrender her name.
She doesn't just angle the grow lights the tenant
nearby paying interest to the UDA
shark crashing together brain bleeds
I screamed pressing my pupil
onto the pane, soft impossible petrichor:
I had me fall into a senseless scripted immobility.
　　　　　Whatever suggestion, I was
impossible banging on the ceiling gas case
plan checklist to move raise the right hand
into the path the lung pump hope for
fire cuckoos strong focus flames eating
muscular twist gaseous heap sunlight
glimmer eyes popped out foaming
　　　　　four caged flames
bubbled unsleeping, it truly yearns to see
the other end is now the centre made up
as everyone always knew, now back to my story
music to edify my character fades on screen
molestation heart at the shape of the flower
the spider turned pink what you deadly on trial
profess will ticket stamp, cold fusion, entry
　　　　　point deliver us: Straight. In the hands
we can grant clerical warrant good cultured

music into the eyes, well, beyond them, to the side,
back and forth in cracked sonata
form you have to put your mental health
first can you imagine fire like blood
run through muscle?
Power acts on this picture:
                    Two sliders droning on an open heart
told to shirk in provident slack corrupted,
blamed; ignition, whole, in the water.
Aqualung. Iron lung. Beef lung. Lung
occasionally. Fair. We ran up the bends,
the river, I can remember, took forceful chunks
out of the sandy banks. We would hide
under the big leaves. Her eyes and mine
                    cyan, later darkening to green
a dot freckle on the pupil of the right
where spring pale creeps back fading
to the centre, into the dark
we'd never have thought in our freest friendship
staring at that bloated toad
its skin rippling with maggots
the whole of focus would land here;
                    the final cuckooed unit
keeping cousins from the oven,
remember that image, that strong central image
from a Sunday film grizzled men
climbing out of the cooker covered
in patches of dirt, sweating,
muscular, heroic:
Just like that. See
                    it. Please.
Could the foreman mark it on a cardboard sign.
The image is strong. They'll get it. The oven.

186

The little children hid beneath the big leaves:
Gunera! In winter the risk seemed severe. Shannon.
Very rough, occasionally rough in far east Lily
and Freddie and Thames and Lily and Phone
and John and Angela and Boat. For someone to hear
                    as the lightning bludgeoned his eyes
people were eating there they were taken away, both eyes,
and he bit through his tongue like rubberised fire
they don't stop eating, awake and moving their jaws
team members, on the floor going through bits of the eye
to discover hints of glimmering blue
and even the almost impossible freckle.
She wouldn't hand over her number
                    evening seminars
hurt me that way if you like, underneath the leaf
riverbed open heart zip up the point is
they walk down the gangway neither unseen
nearly as much coughed up, enough
thousands desiring the crest of destroyed human
remains to stretch up mountainous obscene
this to those is beauty's ideal way down the line
                    flashes of red of its task force
abandon the few who got to have a go no way out
feet along. Cuckoo. Cuckoo. Red flare now, stop it
something enough won't be done.
Perhaps that's where the boy's
own immortality quest had its house
in order. Very care, on and off the plank
over bacterial limits a distant gas
                    wanted to live forever
see that there you, bobbing head, spectacled
blinking in the sunroof
station platform

next to his cases, all alone: Try that
nodded the commission. The safety
shower who splits out at a heat
intensity not to abrase the flesh
                    casket tugging the rods
go onboard to the gym. Continental foods.
That's a powder put in the fridge
to make it thicken. This officer.
Through the tile. Not on fire.
With a stiffy. Here are my dreams:
A temporary status
guidance pack
                    for not living forever.

Inertia Cuckoo

Impossible, again. Shame circled the bath.
Poisoned, for it had one name.
       The way it climbs in the discourse
       enforced before it's dressed.
Memory flaked on bad weed, good arrows,
stoked for the weekend. That song was a spirit
bomb urging us, be peaceful. Walk
through the world answering all of the questions.
       That lung, lung. Occasionally poor.
       There was the type of shame that made you still,
please, saying children to beautiful people
doesn't work either.
Get off the dial and stand a long way back,
the two sliding heart-bits coming to life
       swayed this way and that droning, like the river.
       Could never forget that smell insects refused
their lunch forced out on the water
at spawning night's eve to prance
through a Degas mist imagining their feet
all curled up on his cheeks and eyes in a private view
       killing floor mustn't keep piping up like this
       when people are trying to listen.
Reaching along the aisle with my brainwaves
I told you that it would be alright, and that I'd stay,
and now I know that the cast was a subterfuge.
For that I feel wanted enough though
       the drive to keep me was the same
       that put all the horses back on the shelf
in coloured lines near to the palace back home.
It was a kind of love too, I wonder.

Out Ethics

Jarred this section of land or on the island
doing something wrong came into focus. Doing
                something upsetting, really harmful, like we do
                when we're looking or not looking
at each other into the freckle by the retina displaced
how wrongly it can be lived. Hide for fun under the big leaf.
Weights of certain hypocrisies back for revenge
live scripted in that water ride, want with me for that.
                It may be I would never fall certain again.
                Thinking the shoddy outboard churned the silt
would never catch a fish; not that
going back to the boathouse inland repair shop
needed to happen in public but you'd used that Triad
Cuckoo farm for fourteen years now
                and it was, you'd say, impossible.
                I asked you, and you said that
you can stop buying it but can't can stop being buying
it why anyway in severe pain goes on examination
or no pressure is what took me into exile, gas.
A note of strawberry, or something else,
                something flooding the palate. Water so clear
                you could eat your insect off it. And we did.
We ate everything. We weren't encouraged to stop
eating, well a little, at the right times,
but generally to go on and on and on at it
with all of our rights in tact, later threat,
                later, threat, but for now listen be careful
                who it is who's got the lease on your flat
because it could be the IRA or someone
equally disadvantageous when you lose work
and do try to come home sometime,
won't you, that lung scares me; its gangway
                on the news; its number is painted on its back,
                and now you walk.

Weekend Break

Self poisoned, the architecture
of the Father she fled
amid the impulse pattern
          chosen attacks cruelly
focussed settle down now then to child
then to parent. Dusk, my driven
love found us out, down the stupid
          gangway cracks muted,
please, show me to my desk
the take-home wage, deflecting
these people are going to suffer
          ingrates slacking rue
the day. Put on the sweater
up the flowers, here you are, my sweet
but I am afraid, having always
          strange tracks hewn
moved in predictable circles, numbers
and raised in a good home,
her face turned deadly pale.
          Taking a long breath,
The bed,
I lay awake,
at work we all three sleep in is where my guts
started to repair themselves after the poisoning.
          I was able to dream, free
from the moronic circulation of air that split me up a bit
or drove you away from our bade to scream at
          the pillow for my head is gone
we're technically all here one by one
going to rest a little now

                you keep watch, please,
She can't afford to be known to pass out
the wilderness wherein you live
today, though, it's quiet, a few bunkers
uncovered clean her head
and back down the trail
to the pick-up zone, just a peaceful
walk in the sun remember to stop
                the bleeding, please,
I need this bed to eat us through the earth.
Think back to rest, summer's heart
swell passing through the riverbed,
                floating hair, deep green.

Chivalric Code Red

For this hope stands tiptoe, zephyr
hymnal broken from the throat;
let sing the river rising
adders by the lake,
her chosen family insulation
away from the eye in the sky.
      Ring out shiver ricin
      slow worms next to the pond.
Self employed to fly, migrate
north toward Cliffe to drop there
      eyes white-out, liver
      retched by grass snakes.
Farming all for family
disbanded tattoo memory
      get in, give her ice,
      in a sand lizard hideout,
mindful of airline dog units
mineral water all round
the flag has come to hand.

Punishment

This is true, the narrower gauge
sent water cutting through
the intestines like a knife.
The beautiful holiday come one
again, all fluoride waste heaps
he chonged it back, smiled
        weak as paste
        vacated of all
life in dulled halls
little time
to react he'll tear
them down, friend's bloods
goodly home time arrow
together can't wait today
        it will begin
        so young, seclusion
if we were to flit how would we
divide oh blank it out, my love,
wait and hold fly past
pressed in his ears
power chanced him
to move with nothing
        of the floor
        it all begins
here stay down shut
up. Quieted prison
the property business we built
together wait for that shot each
arm flail crimson,
shut the lights off.

194

                    Child's timeout
                    started to
as you would replace
non sobriety with a pattern
of shots pithy rhyme
alarm colleagues
secure future out
paid with blood together
                    ground, oh ground
                    oh god it is
real the alarms zip clamour
soft insistence at the buzzer
entryway cousins gold tap designer
of the nest her paws on panes
waits to dim the stains
is she there tell them I came.
                    Start the machine
                    early life close
to its, the matter destroyed
flashes assault, smoke
in the sky he toyed
as before run up to dead
stepping back from the roads
bang it let it turn
                    the tooth
                    first words. Signs
staircase crushed she rammed
her elbows out and around
hearing a disarmed red mark
doorway pain grade translating
boy would burst the ceiling
echoing, his dead blood
                    useless, the name

                    on a tag, morning
for his day fell away annoyed
he was yes powerful
timeless more than enough
those that self arranged
where flew they creak tower
burn, enough to bear arms
                    shall begin to
                    exclude from blood
their power, our power,
known, even paid for, how?
We share a meter the black cable
douse it blue interceptor
fixed round a pipe;
oven cooked men in memory
                    they begin
                    to stare now, draft excluder.
Mellified chaplain all
faces glowed and gleamed
sixty. Immunised gut,
where her body
happens to be a schoolboy
trick on anybody
                    who is willing
                    to play, how faster
it failed altogether
dead man survived
cull new deliveries,
he leaves behind
setup challenge no vacuum
upset and annoyed
                    well armed now mount
                    a serious concern, top

up the meter at the corner shop
laughter and nerves amount
to treason what happened next
was the nurses who had had it
up to here with being kicked
at prestige car hire, kicked
                    to twilight, relativity
                    recommended acceptance
electrical specialists plug directly
into the hallway. He exploded
garbage fanfare stop drinking
he bellowed I need your piss test
thudding on the wall.
This too, will pass, not
                    sport blow the whistle
                    twilight cracks of
deferred, missing a storm
spread across the air
hallways snowing heart
swell's return shone back
to the counter still this is, she said,
grow freedom's dreaming rapid at
                    still night. Then there
comes sing the hospital alarm call
seize and comes alarm to sing out sing
hospital junk would break knockout
that freak sing by the car, parked garage
drink sing sing rope She thought the alarm
in desperate repose still there comes the alarm
that sing knock the fuck counter to detail sing break knock
listen floor of junk, by the carpark,
parked hospital recovery bed nets nothing fuck
counter to sing. Sing rope under mattress tyre

sing park details part news making alarm to come sing alarm
come sing alarm junk by the carpark knockout that freak
alarm nets a preferred pipe junk for joint details come the alarm,
                    sing still the alarm at night come
details alarm cracks deferred, missing a storm
spread across the air hall knockout snowing
heart return impossible the hospital alarm call seize
                   sing seize knock junk
sing rope sing under rope under mattress piss
on sing desperate sung rope
under snowing heart to fuck counter sing.
She thought the alarm knockout
that freak bed nets nothing sing counter.
To fuck to sing knock
across dreaming rapid at still night there then junk would break knock
              knock out break sing rope meadow alarms of
flowers sing part making the news up to alarm detail hospital at
night the alarm would call that freak to knockout, sing that thought
alarm one junk still sing to counter to fuck blue flowers
at night alarm to sing the life knocked out the hospital by night.

Calling for Home

Count down from twenty. We returned to night
scented stock. In the bathroom I saw me on the floor
of your life's thought for a moment love cascades
down the generations going to the cabinet adjusting
the ambient humidity. We were quite alone, now,
after the careful intervention I was brought
an interpreter who I came to understand
                would help us with my story.
On the dual carriageway running for your life
the silk's not broken, it's designed to stretch
and contract counting emissions exculpates
support staff. Sixteen. He noted everything down
spoke your voice softly, and in his report
the truth of kind bled out: Not live
in the words but in who they're spoken to, eleven,
                shares in protection. Outside
the secure unit the relatives gathered;
false widows on executive pay her smile a flower,
her voice the song of jade four object constancy
and if I do not survive the poison, it may
be too late, escort her by night
through a secret portal into a windowless world.
No restaurants, video shops, flowering
                seams, for example if this continues
no one will say her 'face, a moon' if there is
no face. The haunted heart of the starbase,
if it had decomposed...

Its Home

(2024)

I need you to have travelled
repellent, or recapture
over and over
where is Anna? What have I made,
to have moved so even
you are obscure, or,
what is left? Am I harmful
at that measure
our painful distance do I go
as Lara dies silent though
I saw your face quite clearly
and so many catastrophes
haunt my train...

Can you say goodnight, or some kindness
so scattered objects helplessly
clawing towards them, which is farther,
testing and pushing and breaking
in the bearing; which was lost
one by one on long car journeys
they waited for you with arms
wide open, as you slowly disappeared.

There's an intercom beside the bed
"its home" it said,
but last night it cut into
my nightmares, Aquila
and the little lamp ahead.

Its home, alkali—the night
stretched out, Aquila
and somebody find us
here in this little room,
little buried room
without a name.

How do they find us
　　at this end
either left across
　　the motorway
mast the radiator works
　　always use the footpath
in this my hollow
　　overground room
the night
　　beckoned to
the sandbags
　　cover and curtain,
its home.

Where the track becomes
the pathway, somehow
she was taken off
the track.
Its home, it yawns
at the mouth of the track
inviting you, wake up.
It entered all my dreams.

Out in the yard the sound seemed to come
the stained glass lantern I could see
to my west ahead of me and my function
at night was to wake and dream.
As any ordinary night I would scream myself awake.

Courage, it is home, took you
my work bed into its arms.
Suddenly, one trembling night
where wakefulness would hurt
time spread down the track,
stared along with lovely heart
a bird warbled to the east of my bed,
my back and song were one.

A fertile sound to the south
of the night watch I lay
pleasant and undisturbed
she was pinned to the floor
and squares of home lit gently
gathering silhouettes
they forced her arm
as she cried out fresh
in the warmth of its home
and tidy the lamplight
auburn I waited
as they took her into the night
lying for all our helplessness.

Laid out on the track
my nights stretched off
as your dusk we recovered,
we recovered, we went home.

Alone, misted the day
oval precinct, missing
as shadows its
fall pretends its home
cantering far off, warmly.

Its home: The heart's revolutions.
Awake and falling silently to sleep.
Some fragrant noise reworked, she stared
backwards into the dusk of its room
alone, its home and waking night
I borrowed from the mist and lost the heart.

I was never meant to lie here, its home
love and money wasted into my pathway
a great future comfort
crossed its home precarity, sense
of under belonging necklace
foot you in the head.

Carried by the home today
to where a tiny signal,
a flickering light
across the divide.
It is my own shadow
some years ago, I see it,
my ghost at the distant window
where I would stand
wrapped in the curtain
observed from the world behind
signalling over the divide with my light
as our city fell dark and quiet,
fearful yet wrapped
in a peculiar sense
that as the hush fell
the dark squares may respond.

There was a kind of garden
and as the lamp of the rose
threw down her light
would we harden our pace?

As silence blew into the city
and the birdsong tended their homes
the dead shall walk, no
dead quiet strange city silt

I must go now
to speak with the lamplight
forty four windows,
more, reply reply reply.

Its home. The sound as they settled was of throats
a gaping open passageway gurgling blackened blood;
the room in the glare of day rang with its slap
a flogged hyde echoed they found their settling silence
redecorated, altered the energies of the space
so the seven corpses arranged about the living
area sat up; dusted themselves down
and began to go about the stations of the home:
You can easily forget them even as they are
right there before you loud, bald in lamplight
seeing or being awake all the way, in wanton disaffection.

Are you the bedside lamp,
  for our rarest love
smarting and pouring out flowers
  ponies inside the brilliant white clouds
the patter of rain on lilypads
  perfect and obscure
remarking on patterns
  arpeggios rising sickness
camped by the solar plexus
  awaiting the primed second
to bring forth my fist
  and crush the air from his misery
so I could kiss his mouth
  and make my home, indentured,
wake up once more to turn you
  over, wiping the blood
from my fingers, and after six
  months on the front line
claim my pardon by this light,
  the will of God.

Wide awake, churned up
  in dream logic
you said the truth
  couldn't harm you
yet I have the feeling
  I'm attending
a lynching party.
  Tell them you had
no choice, in the seat
  beside my bed you sat
to cease to take the names
  I keep my pledge
I was not called.

A cluster of crickets chirruped
at the foot of the stems.
We cupped our ears
burning stakes
practising the next movement
like my rose my heart's
song forever, tiny, prominent
in this room.

Further, higher up, just below the canopy
a mantis held a living body in each arm,
a cricket with a hole in its face
and their beautiful song, of mourning

perhaps or futile aggression
defence psalms, discerning
the character, the glee we imposed
the wall of the little room came through

and a husband and two wives
stepped into the sunny dust cloud,
detecting the threat,
a grandparent at the table.

Hunched over it was clear
they opened up his face
and the children began to sing out
naked threats, a bulge in a jumper

so they aimed around the hearts nullified
on the shoreline canopy of the world
she stood by the ocean, opened
her settling heart, the coast they don't deserve.

Its home. From this tiny room
I saw her too, dragged from her love
spat on, dead in her dance clothes
on the back of the truck
the single ear at the heart
of her chest, still as the moment
before the alarm
took me, its home, you need us
to hate this first,
before the rest of it flowers
under the staining light
from the glass disordered
heart, to prove this faith;
love embraces me, the lamplight
dreaming quarters.

230

Goodbye, Betty, while you're away, know that
we were here, Out and into the garden
to pause and say that, we were here,
to the ever present face vanishing away that we

once were here; the ghosts that step on, becoming
that occasional sound, clear, when the room
is empty and alone there it is:
A single thump, or cracking glass

or of late the sound of my own name spoken
once through the dark neither unresting nor kind
but gestures from a world tread before, we were here
and buried a piece of ourselves.

Index of Titles or First Lines

Acknowlegements

Some of the poems in this book previously appeared in *Granta*, *Cambridge Literary Review*, *The New York Times*, *Poetry Review*, *Devil Tower*, *100 Queer Poems* (Vintage, Penguin) and *Fatberg*. My thanks to the editors.

Songs of the Morning was previously published in pamphlet by Slub Press, London, with thanks to Owen Fortunato Brakspear. *Coronelles Set 1* was published in pamphlet by Veer2, London, with thanks to Rob Kiely.

The images for the two sets of Coronelles, 'Red Admiral' and 'Pipistrell', were drawn by Aubrey Smith.

All photographs are by the author.

The North Road Songbook

© Verity Spott, 2024

Published by Pilot Press, London

ISBN 978-1-7393649-7-7

Typeset by Ian Heames

Printed on 100% recycled paper